SHOHEI OHTANI

CHARLIE BEATTIE

WWW.APEXEDITIONS.COM

Apex is distributed by North Star Editions:
sales@northstareditions.com | 888-417-0195

Produced for Apex by Red Line Editorial.

Photographs ©: Brian Rothmuller/Icon Sportswire/AP Images, cover, 1; Megan Briggs/Getty Images Sport/Getty Images, 4–5; Kyodo/Newscom, 6–7, 12–13, 14–15, 18–19, 20–21, 24–25, 26–27, 28–29, 30–31, 54–55; iStockphoto, 8–9; Kunihiko Miura/The Yomiuri Shimbun/AP Images, 10–11; Chung Sung-Jun/Getty Images Sport/Getty Images, 16–17; Atsushi Tomura/Getty Images Sport/Getty Images, 22–23; Joe Scarnici/Getty Images Sport/Getty Images, 32–33; New York Times Co./Archive Photos/Getty Images, 34–35; Victor Decolongon/Getty Images Sport/Getty Images, 37; Nick Wosika/Icon Sportswire/AP Images, 38–39, 58–59; Jayne Kamin-Oncea/Getty Images Sport/Getty Images, 40–41; Shutterstock Images, 42–43; Ronald Martinez/Getty Images Sport/Getty Images, 44–45; Duane Burleson/Getty Images Sport/Getty Images, 46–47; G. Fiume/Getty Images Sport/Getty Images, 49; Sarah Stier/Getty Images Sport/Getty Images, 50–51; Meg Oliphant/Getty Images Sport/Getty Images, 52–53; Kyodonews/ZUMA Press/Newscom, 56–57

Library of Congress Control Number: 2024952002

ISBN
979-8-89250-725-7 (hardcover)
979-8-89250-777-6 (paperback)
979-8-89250-759-2 (ebook pdf)
979-8-89250-743-1 (hosted ebook)

Printed in the United States of America
Mankato, MN
082025

NOTE TO PARENTS AND EDUCATORS

Apex books are designed to build literacy skills in striving readers. Exciting, high-interest content attracts and holds readers' attention. The text is carefully leveled to allow students to achieve success quickly.

TABLE OF CONTENTS

CHAPTER 1

THE 50-50 CLUB

Shohei Ohtani took off sprinting for third base. The Miami Marlins catcher popped up and threw the ball to third. Ohtani slid just under the third baseman's tag. Ohtani was safe. He had just stolen his 50th base of the 2024 season.

Shohei Ohtani slides into third for his 50th stolen base of the 2024 season.

Ohtani hits the ball deep to left field for his 50th home run of 2024.

Ohtani's night was just getting started. In the sixth inning, he blasted a monster home run. The next inning, Ohtani hit another. That was his 50th home run of the season. Ohtani had rewritten the history books. He became the first Major League Baseball (MLB) player with 50 home runs and 50 stolen bases in a single season. And he reached both milestones in the same game.

A GAME TO REMEMBER

Ohtani's 50-50 game took place on September 19, 2024. Many baseball experts said it was one of the greatest performances in the sport's history. Ohtani went 6-for-6 with three home runs. He recorded 10 RBIs and stole two bases. To top it off, the Los Angeles Dodgers won the game 20–4.

CHAPTER 2

YAKYŪ SHŌNEN

Shohei Ohtani was born on July 5, 1994, in Ōshū, Japan. Both of his parents were athletes. Shohei's mother, Kayoko, was a talented badminton player. His father, Toru, was an amateur baseball player.

Ōshū is located in Iwate Prefecture, which is in northern Japan.

Baseball is very popular among boys and girls across Japan.

Shohei's father taught him to play baseball. Shohei quickly became known as a *yakyū shōnen*. That means "baseball boy" in Japanese. Shohei was a talented hitter. He was also the best pitcher on his team. When he was in seventh grade, his team won a championship game. Shohei recorded 17 of the 18 outs on strikeouts.

SHOHEI THE SWIMMER

Shohei was an excellent all-around athlete as a kid. One of his other sports was swimming. One coach talked about Shohei's skills. He said Shohei might have been good enough to swim in the Olympics.

Shohei lived in a small town. In high school, many big-city teams wanted him to join them. But Shohei decided to stay put. He attended a high school near home. Players there lived at the school. They practiced often. They rarely returned home.

RECORD FASTBALL

Shohei had a blazing fastball when he was in high school. In 2012, he threw a pitch 99 miles per hour (160 km/h). At the time, that was a record for Japanese high school players.

Shohei hits a home run for Hanamaki Higashi High School in 2012.

Shohei's coaches were thrilled with how he devoted himself to baseball. Shohei made sure to eat right. He also created a detailed chart to map out his goals.

Off the field, Shohei was quiet and polite. But on the field, he was a fierce competitor. Professional baseball teams began to notice his skills. They were amazed that he was so good at both hitting and pitching.

In addition to pitching, Shohei also played outfield during high school.

CHAPTER 3

A STAR IN JAPAN

Shohei Ohtani wanted to play in MLB straight from high school. Very few players had ever done that. He also wanted to be both a pitcher and a hitter.

Shohei Ohtani batted and pitched during the 2012 18U Baseball World Championship.

Many MLB teams were interested. But players in the big leagues rarely focus on both pitching and hitting. Most MLB teams told Ohtani he would have to choose. He didn't want to do that. So, Ohtani stayed in Japan. He was drafted by the Hokkaido Nippon-Ham Fighters.

TWO-WAY PLAYERS

Baseball's early days featured many two-way stars. But the practice soon died out. Since the 1930s, few players have been great at both pitching and hitting.

Ohtani recorded his first win with the Hokkaido Nippon-Ham Fighters on June 1, 2013.

Ohtani made history in his second year with Hokkaido. In August 2014, he notched his 10th win as a pitcher. In September, he blasted his 10th home run of the season. No player in Japan's Nippon Professional Baseball (NPB) had ever done both before.

NO. 11

While playing for Hokkaido, Ohtani wore jersey No. 11. It was a nod to Japanese star Yu Darvish. Darvish pitched in Japan from 2005 to 2011. Then he joined MLB.

Ohtani hits his 10th home run of the 2014 season with the Fighters.

Ohtani pitches against the MLB All-Stars in November 2014.

Ohtani continued to improve as a hitter. But he was still known mostly as a star pitcher. In the 2014 NPB All-Star Game, he threw a fastball at 100 miles per hour (161 km/h). That set a record for Japanese professional pitchers. Later that year, Ohtani's 101-mile-per-hour (163-km/h) fastball sawed a bat in half.

MLB ALL-STARS

Ohtani first faced MLB players in 2014. The MLB All-Stars played a special series against Japan's national team. Ohtani put on an impressive show. He struck out seven batters in four innings.

Besides Ohtani, only one other NPB pitcher recorded 15 wins in 2015.

Ohtani's pitching got even better during the 2015 season. He finished the season with a 15–5 record. His earned run average (ERA) was 2.24. He also struck out 196 batters. Rarely are pitchers considered for Most Valuable Player (MVP) Awards. But Ohtani was so good in 2015 that he finished third in the voting.

CHAPTER 4

COMING TO AMERICA

By 2016, Ohtani was a superstar in Japan. Fans thought of him as a better pitcher than hitter. But he was about to change that in a big way.

On September 28, 2016, Ohtani pitched a complete-game shutout for Hokkaido.

Ohtani's .322 batting average in 2016 was second in NPB.

Ohtani blasted 22 home runs in 2016. He also earned the designated hitter (DH) spot on the Best Nine. That's a list of NPB's top players.

That same season, Ohtani had an ERA of 1.86. He was also named as the pitcher for the Best Nine. No player had ever made the list as both a pitcher and a hitter.

Ohtani's amazing 2016 season helped Hokkaido reach the Japan Series. This is the championship of NPB. Ohtani hit .375 in six games. Those hits included four doubles. Ohtani's team rallied to win the series 4–2 over the Hiroshima Carp.

WALK-OFF WINNER

Hokkaido lost the first two games of the 2016 Japan Series. The team needed a win in Game 3. Ohtani came up big with three hits. His third hit was a single in the bottom of the 10th inning. The walk-off hit drove in the winning run.

Hokkaido's 2016 championship win was the team's first title in 10 years.

The Los Angeles Angels introduced Ohtani as part of their team in December 2017.

MLB scouts followed Ohtani's every move. They saw he had more than enough talent for MLB. After another strong year in 2017, Ohtani was ready. Any MLB team that wanted to sign Ohtani had to pay Hokkaido $20 million. In the end, Ohtani picked the Los Angeles Angels.

UNLIKELY ANGEL

Ohtani's choice to join the Angels surprised many. The team wasn't expected to be very good. However, the Angels did have Mike Trout. Ohtani was able to play with one of MLB's best players at the time.

Ohtani didn't disappoint in his first MLB season. In 2018, he hit 22 home runs. He was also named American League (AL) Rookie of the Year. An injury stopped him from pitching much. But he became the first player to hit 20 home runs and pitch at least 50 innings since Babe Ruth in 1919.

THE BABE

Many experts compared Ohtani to legendary slugger Babe Ruth. Ruth broke into MLB as a pitcher in 1914. In 1919, he stopped pitching to focus on hitting. Ruth went on to set a record by hitting 714 home runs. He retired in 1935.

In 1934, Babe Ruth played baseball across Japan. That tour helped make professional baseball possible in the country.

IN THE SPOTLIGHT

INSTANT POWER

Ohtani didn't take long to show off his power in an MLB game. On April 3, 2018, he was playing in his third career game. Ohtani blasted a 397-foot (121-m) home run. It was one of three hits for Ohtani that game.

The next day, Ohtani hit another home run in the fifth inning. In the Angels' next game, he homered yet again. That made Ohtani the first Angels rookie to homer in his first three home games.

OHTANI WAS THE SECOND-FASTEST PLAYER IN ANGELS HISTORY TO HIT 20 HOME RUNS.

17

CHAPTER 5

A UNIQUE STAR

Ohtani became an MLB sensation. The only things that slowed him down were injuries. He couldn't pitch at all in 2019 because of an arm problem. And in 2020, he pitched in only two games.

Ohtani slides into third base for a triple during a 2019 game.

Entering the 2021 season, Ohtani had yet to show American fans what he could do as a pitcher. But that year, he put on an incredible show. He went 9–2 as a pitcher. He struck out 156 batters in only 130 ⅓ innings.

A VARIETY OF PITCHES

Ohtani is best known for his fastball. But he throws several other pitches well. His sweeper is another go-to pitch. It moves right to left across the plate. Ohtani also throws a cut fastball and a splitter. He throws a sinker and a curveball, too.

In 2021, opposing batters hit only .207 against Ohtani.

Ohtani was even better as a hitter in 2021. He crushed 46 home runs that season. That nearly matched his 47 home runs from the previous three years combined. Ohtani also led the league with eight triples. He was the clear choice for the 2021 AL MVP Award.

TWO-WAY ALL-STAR

Ohtani made his first MLB All-Star Game in 2021. He became the first MLB player to make it as both a pitcher and a hitter. But that wasn't enough for Ohtani. He was the AL's starting pitcher and leadoff hitter. Ohtani retired the side in the first inning. The AL All-Stars went on to win 5–2.

Tokyo Tower lit up with the Angels' colors when Ohtani won the 2021 AL MVP Award.

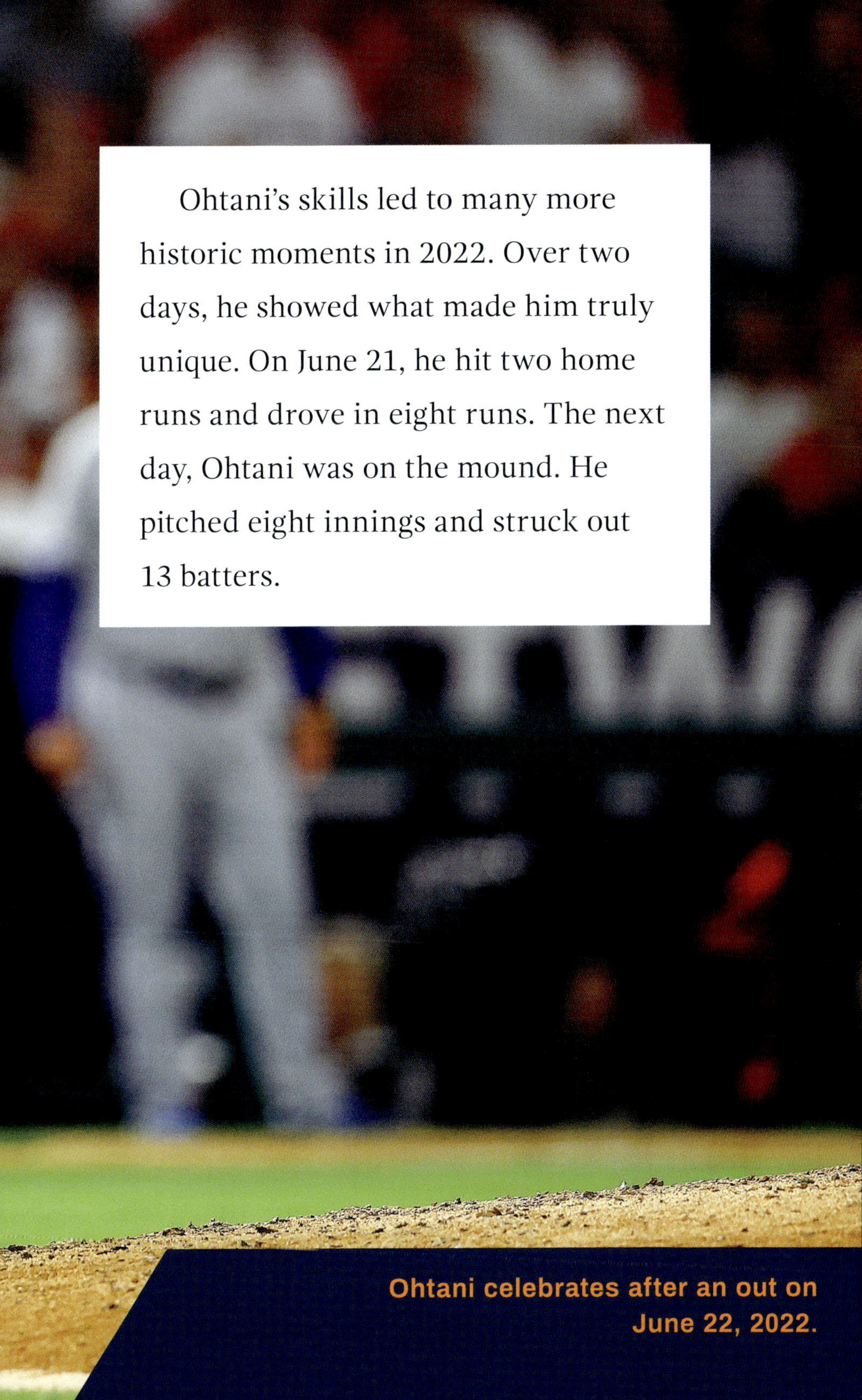

Ohtani's skills led to many more historic moments in 2022. Over two days, he showed what made him truly unique. On June 21, he hit two home runs and drove in eight runs. The next day, Ohtani was on the mound. He pitched eight innings and struck out 13 batters.

Ohtani celebrates after an out on June 22, 2022.

In 2023, Angels players started wearing samurai helmets after hitting home runs in honor of Ohtani.

Despite Ohtani's success, the Angels failed to reach the postseason. The 2023 season was more of the same. Ohtani led the AL with 44 home runs. He also won 10 games as a pitcher. But the Angels struggled. Ohtani's contract was up at the end of the season. Baseball fans wondered where he would go.

SUPERSTAR SHOWDOWN

Japan faced the United States in the final of the 2023 World Baseball Classic. Japan led 3–2 in the ninth. Ohtani was pitching against his Angels teammate Mike Trout. On six pitches, Ohtani struck out Trout to win the game.

THE CYCLE

On June 13, 2019, the Angels faced the Tampa Bay Rays. Ohtani homered in the first inning. In his next at-bat, he doubled to left field. Then the power went out at Tampa Bay's stadium for a half hour.

The stoppage didn't slow Ohtani. Once power was restored, he slapped a ball down the right-field line in his next at-bat. Then he raced around the bags for a triple. Finally, in the seventh inning, Ohtani singled. That made him the first Japanese player to hit for the cycle in an MLB game.

OHTANI WAS ONE OF SIX MLB PLAYERS TO HIT FOR THE CYCLE IN 2019.

CHAPTER 6

A BIG DEAL

By the winter of 2023, Ohtani was baseball's biggest star. He was also a free agent. That meant he could sign with any team. Many fans wondered how big his next contract would be. The deal he signed blew everyone away.

Ohtani celebrates winning his second MVP Award in the 2023 offseason.

The Los Angeles Dodgers gave Ohtani the biggest contract in American sports history. They agreed to pay him $700 million for 10 seasons. Ohtani wasn't switching cities. But he was moving to the National League (NL).

MORE BIG NEWS

Ohtani's big contract wasn't his only event of the 2023 offseason. He also got married. At first, he kept his wife's identity a secret. In February 2024, he announced that she was Mamiko Tanaka. She was a basketball star in Japan.

Ohtani signed with the Los Angeles Dodgers in December 2023.

In August 2024, Ohtani hit a walk-off grand slam for his 40th home run of the season.

Another injury meant Ohtani would not be able to pitch in 2024. But the Dodgers didn't mind. His hitting made him worth the money. He led the NL in runs, RBIs, and home runs. He batted .310 and stole 59 bases. That's why it was no surprise when Ohtani earned his third MVP Award in four years.

SCANDAL

Ohtani uses an interpreter to help him communicate with English speakers. For years, it was Ippei Mizuhara. But in 2024, Mizuhara was charged with stealing money from Ohtani. Mizuhara pleaded guilty to stealing nearly $17 million to cover gambling losses.

Ohtani runs onto the field to celebrate after the Dodgers won the 2024 World Series.

The 2024 season was special for another reason. After seven years in MLB, Ohtani finally reached his first postseason. The Dodgers made it all the way to the World Series. They beat the New York Yankees in five games. Ohtani was a World Series champion! Dodgers fans couldn't wait to see Ohtani bring them even more glory.

TIMELINE

1994

Shohei Ohtani is born in Ōshū, Japan.

2012

Ohtani signs with the Hokkaido Nippon-Ham Fighters of Japan's Nippon Professional Baseball.

2014

Ohtani sets a Japanese record by throwing a 101-mile-per-hour (161-km/h) pitch.

2016

Ohtani helps Hokkaido win the Japan Series by hitting .375 with four doubles in six games.

2017

Ohtani signs with the Los Angeles Angels.

2018: Ohtani hits his first MLB home run in just his third game.

2019: Ohtani becomes the first Japanese player to hit for the cycle in an MLB game.

2021: Ohtani is named AL MVP after hitting 46 home runs and finishing 9–2 as a pitcher.

2023: Ohtani signs a 10-year, $700 million contract with the Los Angeles Dodgers.

2024: Ohtani wins his first World Series title with the Dodgers.

COMPREHENSION QUESTIONS

Write your answers on a separate piece of paper.

1. Write a paragraph that explains the main ideas of Chapter 3.

2. What do you think is the most incredible feat of Shohei Ohtani's career? Why?

3. Which MLB great is Ohtani often compared to?

- A. Yu Darvish
- B. Mike Trout
- C. Babe Ruth

4. Why did Ohtani sign with the Hokkaido Nippon-Ham Fighters after high school?

- A. The team gave him more money than MLB teams.
- B. The team allowed him to both hit and pitch.
- C. The team didn't let him leave Japan.

5. What does **two-way** mean in this book?

Baseball's early days featured many ***two-way*** *stars. But the practice soon died out. Since the 1930s, few players have been great at both pitching and hitting.*

- A. a player who pitches and is good at hitting
- B. a player from before the 1930s
- C. a player who is great without practicing

6. What does **scouts** mean in this book?

MLB ***scouts*** *followed Ohtani's every move. They saw he had more than enough talent for MLB.*

- A. police who keep stadiums safe
- B. fans who love more than one team
- C. people who look for skilled players

Answer key on page 64.

GLOSSARY

amateur
Having to do with playing a sport without getting paid.

contract
An agreement to pay someone money, often for doing work.

cycle
When a player hits a single, double, triple, and home run in the same game.

drafted
Chosen by a team when entering a sports league.

fastball
A pitch thrown at a pitcher's top speed.

free agent
A professional athlete who doesn't have a contract with a team and is free to sign with any team.

interpreter
Someone who can speak two or more languages and helps people understand one another.

postseason
A set of games played after the regular season to decide which team is the champion.

rookie
An athlete in his or her first year as a professional player.

walk-off
A play that ends a game by scoring a run.

TO LEARN MORE

BOOKS

Buckley, James, Jr. *Who Is Shohei Ohtani?* Penguin Workshop, 2025.

Kim, Cheryl. *Shohei Ohtani: Baseball Trailblazer.* Capstone Press, 2024.

Tischler, Joe. *Shohei Ohtani.* Amicus Learning, 2025.

ONLINE RESOURCES

Visit **www.apexeditions.com** to find links and resources related to this title.

ABOUT THE AUTHOR

Charlie Beattie is a writer and former sportscaster. Originally from St. Paul, Minnesota, he now lives in Charleston, South Carolina, with his family.

INDEX

ANSWER KEY:

1. Answers will vary; 2. Answers will vary; 3. C; 4. B; 5. A; 6. C